LIFE IN THE PAST

ANCIENT GREECE

Jane Bingham

Adapted from an original text by Stewart Ross

FRANKLIN WATTS
LONDON•SYDNEY

First published in 2009 by Franklin Watts

Franklin Watts
338 Euston Road
London NW1 3BH

Franklin Watts Australia
Level 17/207 Kent Street, Sydney, NSW 2000

Produced by Arcturus Publishing Limited,
26/27 Bickels Yard, 151–153 Bermondsey Street, London SE1 3HA

Life in the Past is based on the series *Rich and Poor*, published by Franklin Watts.

Editor: Alex Woolf
Designer: Tim Mayer and Mike Reynolds
Illustrator: Adam Hook
Picture researcher: Glass Onion Pictures

Picture Credits
Art Archive: 7 (Dagli Orti), 8 (Kanellopoulos Museum, Athens / Dagli Orti), 9 (National Archaeological Museum, Athens / Dagli Orti), 10 (Soprintendenza Archaeologica Salerno / Dagli Orti), 11 (British Museum / Eileen Tweedy), 12 (Archaeological Museum, Istanbul / Dagli Orti), 13 (Archaeological Museum, Thebes / Dagli Orti), 14 (National Archaeological Museum, Athens / Dagli Orti), 15 (Museo Nazionale Palazzo Altemps, Rome / Dagli Orti), 16 (Musée du Louvre, Paris / Dagli Orti), 18 (Musée du Louvre, Paris / Dagli Orti), 19 (Musée du Loubre, Paris / Dagli Orti), 20 (Museo Nazionale, Taranto / Dagli Orti [A]), 21 (Museo Nazonale, Taranto / Dagli Orti), 26 (Dagli Orti), 27 (Archaeological Museum, Ferrara / Dagli Orti), 28 (National Archaeological Museum, Athens / Dagli Orti).
Bridgeman Art Library: 4 (Bilarchiv Steffens), 6, 22 (National Archaeological Museum, Athens), 23 (British Museum, London), 24 (Ancient Art and Architecture Collection Ltd).
Shutterstock: cover (Rob Lilley).

A CIP catalogue record for this book is available from the British Library.

Dewey Decimal Classification Number: 938

ISBN 978 0 7496 9044 1

Printed in China

Franklin Watts is a division of Hachette Children's Books, an Hachette UK Company
www.hachette.co.uk

· CONTENTS ·

The Haves...

Ancient Greece was not one country. It was a collection of **city states**. City states were independent cities surrounded by land.

The most important city states were Athens and Sparta. They were both very rich and powerful.

Citizens

In the city states there were two main groups of people – citizens and everybody else. Citizens had some important rights. For example, they had the right to a fair trial. They were usually wealthy too.

Now the ancient Acropolis (upper city) of Athens is in ruins, but it was once magnificent.

... and the Have-Nots

Non-citizens were divided into two groups: the free and the unfree. The free were made up of two kinds of people. First, there were people from the region who were not citizens. Second, there were outsiders who came from other regions.

Golden Touch

The Greeks knew that money could not buy happiness. They told the story of Midas, who wished that everything he touched would turn into gold:

'Midas soon begged to be released from his wish, because he was fast dying of hunger and thirst.'

From *Greek Myths* by Robert Graves

Slaves

The unfree were slaves. Most of them came from outside Greece. Some slaves had comfortable lives. Others worked very long hours and died young.

A female slave helps her mistress to dress.

5

Palaces and Dorms

Some wealthy Greeks had two homes: a town house and a villa in the country. Town houses were built around a courtyard. On the upper floor, there were rooms for women only.

Country houses were more spread out than town houses. They usually had just one floor.

Soldiers' Barracks

In Sparta, young male citizens lived together in soldiers' **barracks**. This was to make them tough and disciplined. They slept in dormitories and ate in a large dining room.

This is the royal palace at Knossos, on the Greek island of Crete. It is larger than two football pitches.

Cottages and Caves

Rich people's homes were often built from stone. These ruined houses are on the island of Delos.

Flats and Houses

Some people in Athens lived in flats. The Greek writer Aeschines wrote:

'**Synoika** *is the name by which we call a residence shared among a number of rent-payers, while ...* **oika** *denotes a house occupied by one family only.*'

Quoted in *Daily Life in Ancient Greece at the Time of Pericles* by Robert Flacelière

Poor people in Athens lived in very small houses. Their houses had flat roofs and small windows. Some homes were carved out of rock.

Household slaves lived in their master's house. But many slaves had no real home. They slept together in crowded, dirty buildings.

Pops is Boss

In ancient Greek families, the husband was in charge. His wife and children had to obey him.

Wealthy women spent most of their time at home. They ran the household and gave orders to their slaves.

Separate Lives

In Sparta, most men belonged to the army. Their wives were left to run the family home and lands.

Girls helped their mothers, but boys left home at the age of seven. They lived in soldiers' barracks and rarely saw their parents.

A Greek bride and groom are carried home in a special chariot.

Working Together

This clay model shows a poor woman at work.

In poorer Greek families, wives often helped their husbands with their work. Usually the children helped as well. In the countryside, wives and children had a range of tasks. They helped look after the animals and harvest the crops.

Married Life

Wealthy Greek couples usually had an arranged marriage. Their parents chose a partner from another rich family.

Poorer Greeks sometimes married for love. Many slaves had no chance of a proper family life.

Left to Die

The Spartans only wanted strong children. The writer Plutarch said:

'They examined the child: … if it was sickly or misshapen, they had it taken to a high cliff [where it was left to die].'

Quoted in *Daily Life in Ancient Greece at the Time of Pericles* by Robert Flacelière

Rich Robes

Most Greek clothes were made from wool. Only the rich could afford cotton or silk. The clothes of both the rich and poor were loose and simple.

The usual dress for men was a short tunic, called a **chiton**. In cold weather, men wore a woollen cloak.

Women's Wear

Well-off women wore a **peplos**. This was a large rectangle of cloth that could be pinned in a number of ways.

Rich women wore lots of jewellery. They also used make-up and dyed their hair.

Greek jewellery was often made from gold. Women wore bracelets, earrings, necklaces and anklets.

Bare and Simple

Poorer men and women dressed in simple tunics. Most of them could not afford shoes.

In hot weather, male workers wore a loincloth. This was a strip of cloth tied around the waist. Sometimes they wore no clothes at all.

No Clothes

The Greeks were not embarrassed by the male body. In Greek art, men are often shown in the nude.

A Woman's Complaint

Some rich women hated spending time on their appearance. In the play *Lysistrata*, a woman complains:

'What could we ever do that was any use? Sitting at home putting flowers in our hair, putting on cosmetics and saffron gowns?'

From *Lysistrata* by Aristophanes

Some men wore an *exomis*. This was a tunic that hung from one shoulder.

Healthy Eating

'Bring me wine!' This carving shows a rich man enjoying a feast.

Rich Greeks enjoyed a healthy diet. They ate plenty of bread and green vegetables, as well as beans, lentils, garlic, cheese and onions. They also had a range of meat and fish to choose from. Meals were washed down with wine, often mixed with water.

Dinner Parties

Wealthy men in Athens met for dinner parties. The guests lay on couches and the food was served on low tables.

Entertaining Dinners

The writer Xenophon described the entertainment at a dinner party:

'At this moment the girl began to play on her flute … she took [12 hoops] and threw them spinning up into the air as she danced.'

From *The Symposium* by Xenophon

Empty Tummies

Poor people ate bread for most meals. Sometimes the price of bread rose very high. Then many poor people went hungry.

Cheese and fish were quite cheap to buy. Meat and green vegetables were expensive. Most poor people drank water, but it was not always clean.

All farming families made their own cheese. This man is grating cheese into a bowl.

Olives

All Greek people ate olives. They also crushed the olives to make oil. Poor people ate chunks of bread dipped in olive oil.

Praying for Health

A doctor cuts a patient's arm to let the blood flow out. The Greeks believed that this would make people better.

When the Greeks fell ill, they prayed to a god for help. They believed that Asklepios, the god of healing, could cure them. Rich people visited the shrine of Asklepios and offered expensive gifts to the god.

Greek Doctors

The Greeks did not just rely on Asklepios. They also had some very good doctors. Greek doctors studied the human body and worked out ways to cure diseases. The leading Greek doctor was Hippocrates. He is known as the 'father of medicine'.

Magic Medicine

Poor people could not afford a doctor. Instead, they relied on magic charms and spells.

Many Greeks believed that snakes had healing powers. People also made medicines from herbs.

In spite of their efforts, many people died of disease. Half of all children died before they were ten. Adults usually died in their 40s and 50s.

Fitness First

The great thinker Socrates wrote:

'The body is involved in all human activities, … it is very important that it should be as fit as possible.'

From *Memoirs of Socrates* by Xenophon

A statue of Asklepios, the god of healing. On his staff is a sacred snake.

Schools for the Rich

Only boys from rich families went to school.
There were no girls' schools. In Athens, boys started
school at seven. They studied reading, writing,
mathematics, music and sport.

Reading and Writing

Pupils had to learn long passages from famous books.
If they did not study hard, their
teachers beat them. Young boys
practised writing on wax tablets.

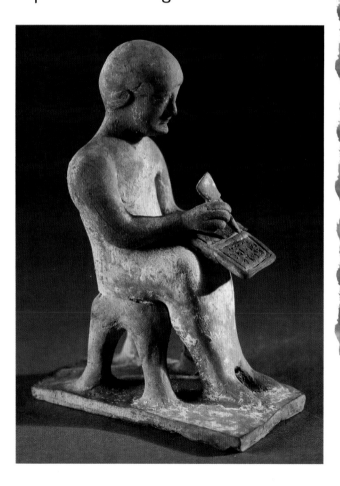

Sweet Music

The Greeks thought everyone
should learn music. The great
thinker Aristotle wrote:

'*The subject is well
adapted to young minds;
for music has a natural
sweetness, and youth is
intolerant of anything
unsweetened.*'

From *Politics* by Aristotle

**This man is writing on a clay
tablet with a sharp stick.**

Learning on the Job

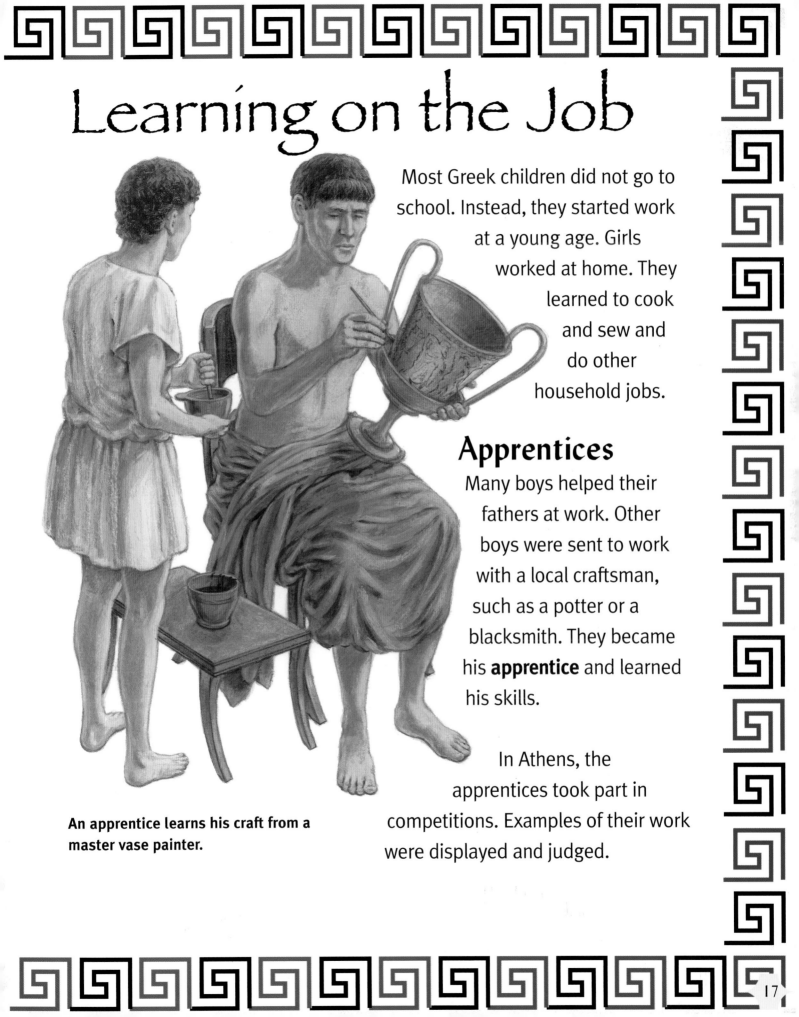

Most Greek children did not go to school. Instead, they started work at a young age. Girls worked at home. They learned to cook and sew and do other household jobs.

Apprentices

Many boys helped their fathers at work. Other boys were sent to work with a local craftsman, such as a potter or a blacksmith. They became his **apprentice** and learned his skills.

In Athens, the apprentices took part in competitions. Examples of their work were displayed and judged.

An apprentice learns his craft from a master vase painter.

Doers and Thinkers

Most male citizens did some kind of work. In Sparta, the men were soldiers. In Athens, many citizens worked as traders. They bought and sold goods such as grain, wine and pottery. Farmers worked hard all year round.

Wealthy Greeks had lots of free time. Some took part in sports and army training. Some used their leisure time to study.

Great Minds

Many great **philosophers** came from ancient Greece. They include Socrates, Plato and Aristotle. Other brilliant Greeks were the mathematician Pythagoras and the scientist Archimedes.

This vase shows two thinkers, or philosophers, sharing their ideas.

Slaves and Criminals

A Greek farmer ploughs his field using a pair of oxen.

All poor Greeks worked when they could. Slaves had no choice. They had to do what their owners wanted. If they did not work well, they were punished.

Trouble in Town

Life was very hard for poor people in towns. If they were ill or lost their job, they could starve. Some people without jobs turned to crime. They survived by robbing others.

Suitable Work

Plato believed that people should stick to the jobs they knew:

'When the cobbler … attempts to force his way into the class of warriors … then this meddling is the ruin of the state.'

From *The Republic* by Plato

Actors and Plays

Wealthy Greeks enjoyed going to the theatre. They watched actors perform comedies and tragedies. All the actors were men. They wore masks to show their characters.

Most Greek plays had only three actors. A large group called the chorus helped to tell the story.

In Athens, there was a drama festival each year. Playwrights competed to write the best play.

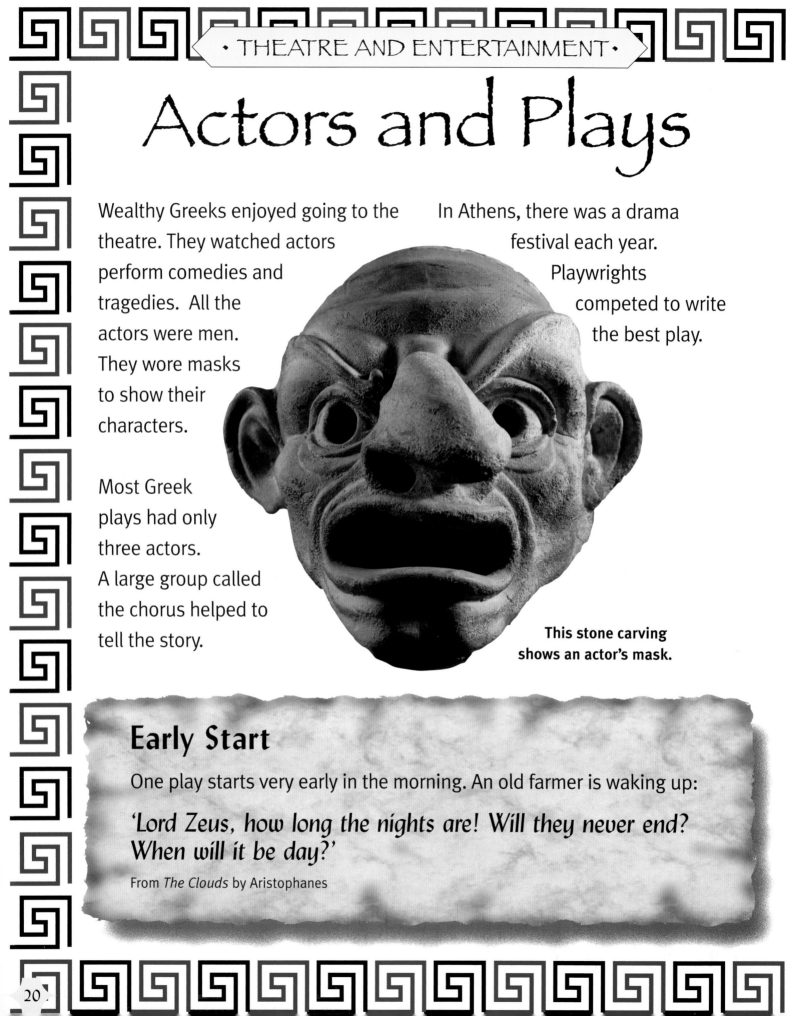

This stone carving shows an actor's mask.

Early Start

One play starts very early in the morning. An old farmer is waking up:

'Lord Zeus, how long the nights are! Will they never end? When will it be day?'

From *The Clouds* by Aristophanes

Party Time!

Poorer people had fun at religious festivals. They joined in the parades and had parties in the streets. People also enjoyed playing ball games and going hunting or fishing.

Myths and Legends

Poor people could not read, but they loved stories. In the winter evenings, people took turns at reciting poems and telling stories. Even the poorest people knew many myths and legends.

The Greeks told wonderful tales about their gods and heroes. One very famous hero was called Heracles. He had to perform twelve impossible tasks.

This painting shows a religious festival in Athens. At the festivals, people sang hymns, played music and danced in the streets.

Amazing Athletes

Wrestling was a popular Olympic sport.

All Greek men tried to stay fit and healthy. Some of them worked out in a public sports centre called the **gymnasium**.

Men and women went to the public baths. They had their bodies washed, scraped clean and oiled by expert slaves.

Olympic Games

Greek athletes competed in a range of events. Sporting events included races, long jumps and throwing the javelin.

The most important contest was the Olympic Games. The Olympics were held every four years at Olympia.

Boys and Women

The poor people of Greece did not have time for athletics. But some young boys were trained as chariot drivers. They competed in very exciting races.

This Spartan girl is taking part in a running race.

No Prizes

Winners at the Olympics were given a wreath of olive leaves. This shocked the Persians, who liked to compete for money. One Persian said:

'What kind of men are these that compete with one another for no material reward, but only for honour!'

From *The Histories* by Herodotus

Super Spartans

Women had their own contests, too. Most of the women's prizes went to the Spartans. Spartan women and girls trained very hard to become strong and fit.

The Rulers ...

Each Greek **city state** had its own method of government. Some states were ruled by kings and some by priests. Sometimes a group of powerful people were in charge. Sparta had two kings, who were controlled by five **magistrates**. The magistrates were elected by the citizens.

Governing Athens

In Athens, all male citizens played a part in running their city. They went to meetings and voted for government officials. Citizens took it in turns to work as an official in the government.

This is where the citizens of Athens met. They had about forty meetings a year.

... and the Ruled

Most Greek people had very few rights. Women and children had to obey their husbands and fathers. Slaves were owned by their masters and mistresses.

The only poor people with any power were the peasant farmers of Athens. They were citizens, so the men in their families had the right to vote.

'Look what you've done!' A slave girl is scolded by her mistress.

Defending Slavery

The Greeks believed it was right to keep slaves. Aristotle wrote:

'It is necessary and practical that some should rule and others be ruled; some people are marked out from birth to be ruled, while others are born to rule.'

From Aristotle's *Politics*

Temples and Priests

The Greeks worshipped many gods and goddesses. Each of the gods had their own shrine or temple.

Rich people gave the gods expensive gifts. They often **sacrificed** a goat or an ox. Poorer people offered smaller gifts, such as honey, olives or corn. They feared the gods would only answer the prayers of the rich.

Oracles

Some priests and priestesses claimed that they could see the future. They were called **oracles**. Rich people paid the oracle to find out what was going to happen.

The most famous oracle lived at Delphi. She had a beautiful temple.

Favourite Gods

Some gods were special favourites of the poor. In the countryside, many people worshipped Pan. He was half-man and half-goat. Dionysus, the god of wine, was another favourite.

In Athens, Demeter was very popular. She was the goddess of crops. Once a year people held a big festival in her honour. Both rich and poor joined in the fun.

The god Dionysus dances with his followers. He is holding a large cup of wine.

Advice from the Oracle

Before the leaders of Thebes fought against Athens, they asked the oracle at Delphi for advice.

The oracle said that they should not act alone. She told them to ask their 'nearest' to help them. From *The Histories* of Herodotus

Doing your Duty

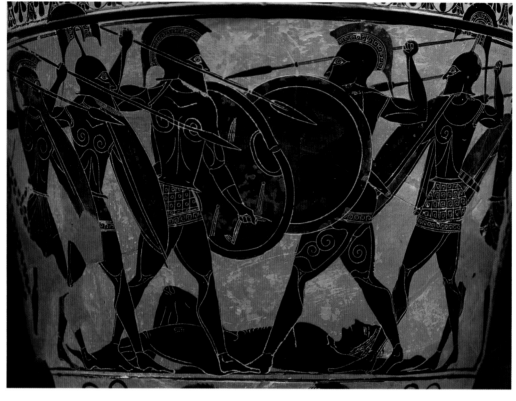

**Greek hoplites wore metal helmets and leg guards.
Some had breastplates to protect their chests.**

All male citizens were expected to fight for their **city state**.
They had to keep fit and have regular training.

Army and Navy

Most Greek soldiers fought on foot.
Greek foot soldiers were called
hoplites. They carried shields and
fought with spears. The best foot
soldiers came from Sparta.

Athens had a great navy. The navy
fought in warships called **triremes**.
These were long wooden ships,
driven by sails and oars.

Making up the Numbers

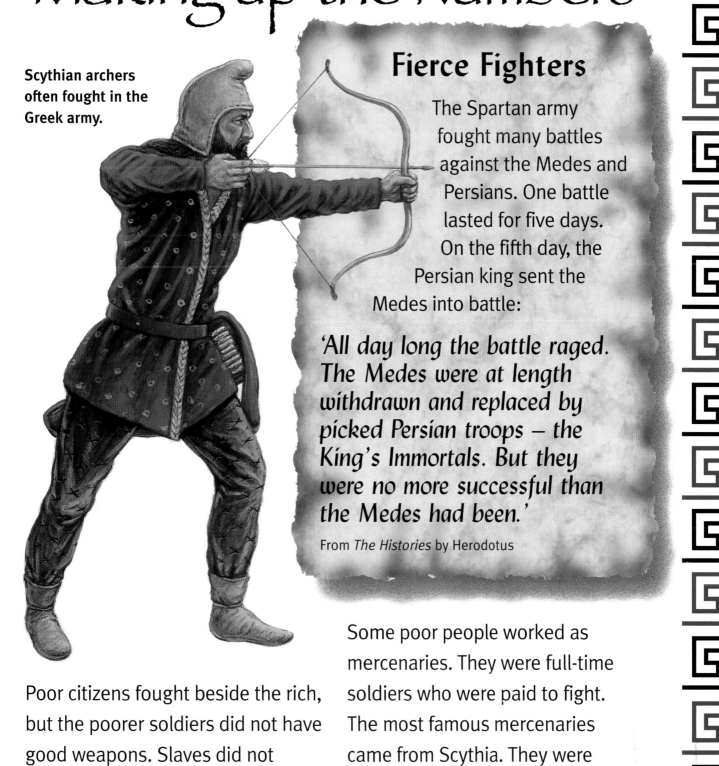

Scythian archers often fought in the Greek army.

Fierce Fighters

The Spartan army fought many battles against the Medes and Persians. One battle lasted for five days. On the fifth day, the Persian king sent the Medes into battle:

'All day long the battle raged. The Medes were at length withdrawn and replaced by picked Persian troops – the King's Immortals. But they were no more successful than the Medes had been.'

From *The Histories* by Herodotus

Poor citizens fought beside the rich, but the poorer soldiers did not have good weapons. Slaves did not usually fight in the army.

Some poor people worked as mercenaries. They were full-time soldiers who were paid to fight. The most famous mercenaries came from Scythia. They were skilled archers.

All dates are BCE

c. 1250	The city of Troy is destroyed.
c. 1200	Invaders from the north, the Dorians, arrive in Greece.
c. 1100	Greeks arrive on the coast of Ionia (modern Turkey). They set up the first Greek overseas cities.
c. 800	The ancient Greek civilization begins.
c.776	The first Olympic Games are held.
c. 750	The Greek alphabet is first used.
c. 750–700	The poet Homer writes the *Iliad* and the *Odyssey*.
c. 705	The first stone buildings in Greece are constructed.
c. 700	The city state of Attica is founded.
c. 650	Classic Greek sculpture is first created.
c. 600	The first Greek coins are circulated.
594	Solon (640–559) introduces changes to the Athenian government.
c.508	Athens begins to be governed by its own citizens.
490–479	The Greeks fight wars with Persia.
490	The Greeks defeat the Persian invaders at the Battle of Marathon.
483	Athens finds a new supply of silver at Laurium.
480	Athens defeats the Persian fleet at the Battle of Salamis.
c. 480	The playwright Euripides is born.
c. 469	Hippocrates, the famous doctor, is born.
462	Pericles introduces political changes in Athens. The 'golden age' of Athens begins with many fine buildings, such as the Parthenon, being constructed.
460–446	Athens fights its first war against Sparta.
c. 460	The historian Thucydides is born.
457	Long Walls are built between Athens and Piraeus.
c. 454	Athens becomes the most powerful city state in Greece.
c. 450	The playwright Aristophanes is born.
431–404	Athens fights its second war against Sparta.
427	The philosopher Plato is born.
404	Athens surrenders to Sparta.
384	The philosopher Aristotle is born.
336–323	Alexander the Great is king of Macedonia, in northern Greece.
c. 287	Archimedes the scientist is born.
146	The Romans conquer the Greeks and Greece becomes part of the Roman Empire.

· FURTHER INFORMATION ·

Books

Ancient Greece by Andrew Solway (Oxford, 2001)

History in Stone: Ancient Greece by Philip Wilkinson (Silver Dolphin, 2001)

Men, Women and Children in Ancient Greece by Colin Hynson (Wayland, 2007)

Picturing the Past: Greece by John Malam (Franklin Watts, 2004)

Virtual History Tours: Look Around A Greek Temple by Richard Dargie (Franklin Watts, 2007)

Websites

www.ancientgreece.com
www.ancientgreece.co.uk
www.historyforkids.org/learn/greeks
www.bbc.co.uk/schools/ancientgreece

apprentice Someone who works with a master craftsman in order to learn the master's skills.

barracks Large buildings where soldiers live.

chiton A tunic worn by Greek men. The *chiton* hung from both shoulders.

city state A city and the lands that surround it.

exomis A tunic worn by Greek men. The *exomis* hung from one shoulder.

gymnasium A kind of sports centre where Greek men exercised and trained to become fit.

hoplite A Greek soldier who fought on foot.

magistrate A government official. Magistrates make sure that people obey the law.

oika A house for one family.

oracle A priest or priestess who claims that he or she can see into the future.

peplos The main piece of clothing worn by Greek women. The *peplos* was a large rectangle of cloth that could be pinned in a number of ways.

philosopher A thinker. Philosophers think very deeply about serious subjects.

sacrifice Kill an animal as an offering to a god or goddess.

symposium A Greek dinner party for men only.

synoika A building that is divided into flats.

trireme A large Greek warship that is driven by oars and sails. Triremes have three decks.

· INDEX ·

Page numbers in **bold** refer to illustrations.